Joy in the Morning

Joy in the Morning

Yes, I remember Steeple Bumpleigh,
The baaing sheep, the lowing beeves,
The chaffering chickens scratching plumply,
The reassuring hand of Jeeves,

Sweet Nobby Hopwood, so good-eggy,
Soul-mate to Boko Fittleworth,
Edwin the boy-scout, dire and dreggy,
Ought to have been put down at birth,

The jealousy of Stilton Cheesewright,
The drippiness of Florence Craye,
The twittering birds and buzzing bees right
Through the unending summer's day,

The loopiness of Uncle Percy,
The ghastliness of Bertie's aunt,
You have to say it's such a mercy –
For Jeeves there's no such word as can't.

Poems by

John Whitworth

Cover: Katie Whitworth

ISBN 13- 978-1-945752-22-3

Kelsay Books
White Violet Press
www.kelsaybooks.com

To Doreen, Ellie, Katie and all the cats

I would also like to make a special dedication to Eratosphere,
a website for poets like me who rhyme and scan.
I have found it of inestimable value

Acknowledgments

Magazines:

Acumen
First Things
Fourteen
Hudson Review
Light
Measure
New Statesman
New Walk
Poetry Review
Quadrant
The Interpreter's House
The New Criterion
The Oldie
The Raintown Review
The Spectator
Trinacria

Anthologies:

Adlestrop Remembered
Funny Haha Funny Peculiar
The Iron Book of Humorous Verse
The Quadrant Book of Poetry 2001-2010
Wicked Poems edited by Roger McGough

'You and the Universe' won the Melbourne Shakespeare Society's 2nd Sonnet Competition.

'Flittermouse' was a runner-up in The Poetry on the Lake Competition 2012.

Some of these poems are from a Pamphlet 'A Poet's Prayer', published by The Gruffyground Press in a limited.signed edition on beautiful paper with an original woodcut at £32. Wow!

Contents

A Coat, a Hat and a Gun

Down these mean streets a man must go who needs
A lot of easy things he hasn't got,
Down these mean streets a man must go who bleeds
To death like other men, except he's not
Like other men, his heart is stouter, stronger
Than yours or mine, that's why he's in a book,
For books are short and sweet, but lives are longer
And few can stand the cool, protracted look
You get with Art, that's why it was invented,
Why Chandler wrote it down and went on writing
Till booze and living killed him, discontented,
Repressed and lonely, all the unexciting
Business of not being Marlowe, not being tough,
Not writing more and better, all that stuff.

A Poet's Prayer

I watch the bastards moving in
To tax my whisky and my gin
And tear me from my life of sin.

Alas that any man should sink,
Enfeebled by the demon drink,
To depths too dire to even think.

Before I tumble on my face
And seal my doom and my disgrace
The Government is on my case.

They beggar me to save my soul
And imitate the Saviour's role
To justify the cash they stole.

Christ, who turned water into wine,
Watch over me and what is mine,
Turn all these devils into swine.

Aphrodisiac Verse

Casanova loves potato.
Chips are what he gives his chick.
Though she be as chaste as Plato
Sizzling chips will do the trick.

What a rhizome, steal some, buy some,
Mother Nature's passion fruit!
Guys from Cuba prize that tuber.
Senoritas dig that root.

Monks in cloisters swear by oysters.
Fatties crave a chocolate bar.
Horn of rhino? You and I know
Here's a food that's better far.

Slice 'em, mash 'em, dice 'em, smash 'em,
Spuds are just the stuff for ladies.
Cold as ice girls, far too nice girls—
Soon they'll be as hot as Hades!

Adlestrop Unwound

I've quite forgotten Adlestrop,
Upper Slaughter, Lower Slaughter,
Foggy Bottom, Devil's Drop,
Faintley-Furtive-in-the-Water,

Squeezegut Alley, Nettlefold,
Bogshole, Chicksands, Chickenshit,
Little-Piddle-on-the-Wold,
Porlock, Warlock, Witch's Tit,

Stinking Bishop. I don't think
I'm happy with a lot of those.
God, I need another drink!
Plumstead, Bumstead, Parson's Nose?

The Leith Police dismisseth us.
Is Leith a place? And where if so?
Carcinoma, Platypus,
Steeple Bastard? I don't know.

All the Things

It isn't what you may have said;
it's rather what you might.
It isn't even what you did;
it's what you didn't quite.
It's how a place is laced with light
and colour when you're in it,
It's how you make an hour hurtle
past me in a minute,
It's how you make, all arsey-versey
and contrariwise,
A minute freeze for ever
in the flicker of your eyes,
Yes, forever and forever in a flicker of your eyes.

You're the silver mines of Saturn,
you're the waterspouts of Venus,
You're the secret name Leviathan
tattooed along his penis,
You're the meekness of a ferret,
you're the cunning of a pigeon,
You're the meaning of the meaning
of the meaning of religion,
The beatitude of being there,
the sanctity of stuff
And the riot of abundance
when too much is not enough,
Such a riot of abundance when too much is not enough.

Like the quintessential nothing
of your absence from a room,
Like the echoes multiplying down
an empty catacomb,

Like the rightness of fried eggs
in their affinity with ham,
Like the rightness of Rhett Butler
when he doesn't give a damn,
Like the love of Marx for cricket,
like the flatulence of Freud,
Like the flocks of chocolate penguins
on a clockwork asteroid,
All those flocks of chocolate penguins on a clockwork asteroid.

Oh, you're fairer than the fairest
of the choristers of Kings,
And you're softer than the feathers
on a cherub's whirring wings,
When you move, you move like Aphrodite
slipping through the waves,
As the sheeted corpses rise in
jubilation from their graves,
When you smile, the smile you smile is
sweeter than the Mona Lisa's.
You're as perfect as a poem
or a parable of Jesus,
Just as perfect as a poem or a parable of Jesus.

Angry Penguin

for Ern Malley from whose complete works
many of these phrases are taken

In the twentyfifth year of my age
I find myself to be a dromedary.
Loose-lipped, imperious, I stalk my cage
In the twentyfifth year of my age,
My bardbrow beetles as I swell with rage,
Robber of dead men's dreams whose eyes are scary,
In the twentyfifth year of my age,
I hubble-bubble like a bloody Mary.

I hubble-bubble, the black swan of trespass
Where urchins pick their noses in the sun.
Mad monks incontinently chant their vespers,
I hubble-bubble, the black swan of trespass
On alien waters, fraught as chinese whispers,
As lights are doused and vanish one by one .
Black as my funeral hat, the swan of trespass
Makes urchins bloom like roses from a gun.

They bloom like roses in the bitter breeze
Like long-shanked Ibises that on the Nile
Unmoving move, a calm immortal frieze
That bloom like noses in the bitter breeze,
The sole clerks of my metamorphoses
Who split the infinite beyond the bile,
Whose long semitic noses in the breeze,
Like souls from leaking roofs define a style.

Autumn Villanelle

Bright day declines. Long shadows grow
Across etiolated grass.
It is the season of the crow.

Tall forests murmur to and fro.
Their yellowing leaves are sick and sparse.
Bright day declines. Long shadows grow

Stinkhorns and polypores below
In the abandoned underpass.
It is the season of the crow.

The mood is lowering, indigo.
Thick fogs descend like clouded glass.
Bright day declines. Long shadows grow.

Your steps are faltering and slow,
For fear of falling on your arse.
It is the season of the crow.

Our dream of summer's golden glow
Has dwindled to an age of brass.
Bright day declines. Long shadows grow.
It is the season of the crow.

Batman Rocks

I come from Gotham City
To say that Batman Rocks!
You can't believe how shitty
Things were in Gotham City.
The brigands and banditti,
The perverts and the pox
Infesting Gotham City
Would scare you from your socks.

All hail the Caped Crusader,
The Guardian of the Good,
Thor's hammer to the raider,
Our steely Caped Crusader,
Enabler and aider,
Our modern Robin Hood,
The saintly Caped Crusader
For God and Motherhood.

The criminal fraternity
Are struck with shock and awe.
They lose their taciturnity,
The criminal fraternity.
And question his paternity
Until their throats are raw,
Cursing for all eternity
The Keeper of the Law.

So I'm up from Gotham City
To tell you Batman's tops!
He hits the nitty-gritty,
So dashing, dark and witty,
The Goth in Gotham city,

With all his groovy props,
So sexy, sweet and pretty,
The popsy of the cops,
　　　He is,
The popsy of the cops!

Black Dogs

I lie awake and think about the past
is a line I stole from the Child Edmund Gosse

It's four o'clock. There's nothing to be done.
Familiar shades are gathering round my bed
To tell me that my earthly race is run.
Black dogs roam up and down inside my head.
The sad, susurrant mammerings of the dead
Oppress my soul and hope is fading fast.
Those fucking dogs are frantic to be fed.
I lie awake and think about the past.

It's four o'clock. There's nothing to be done.
Great rags of birds are perched up on the shed,
Hooded like Druids, waiting for the sun;
Their wingspans make a most impressive spread.
Lately I talk a lot but lose the thread.
The scope for screwing up in spades is vast
And what's to say that's not been better said?
I lie awake and think about the past.

It's four o'clock. There's nothing to be done.
The tanks are rolling down from Birkenhead.
Our Southern cities will be overrun
In days. I've run it through from A to Z.
The Thames will all too soon be running red.
Our enemies are at the gates at last.
My shelves are stacked with documents to shred.
I lie awake and think about the past.

My heart is heavy as a lump of lead.
It beats: THE CHIPS ARE DOWN; THE DIE IS CAST.
So may stones, so very little bread!
I lie awake and think about the past.

Bloater Paste

I sing the joys of bloater paste
On dripping rounds of buttered toast.
Let not a morsel go to waste
For you're the spread I love the most.

In wet and windy days of yore
I sought a place around the fire
I sought your comfort more and more
Of bloater taste I'd never tire.

Bring me my shards of buttered bliss
And greasy little paws to grip 'em
Let unbelievers take the piss.
We are the acolytes of Shippam,

I burn my nightlight at both ends.
What better bliss than this, the taste
Of fish among my childhood friends,
Of sterling Shippam's bloater paste?

Blood Wedding

The bloody footprints down the hall,
The baby bricked into the wall,
The nanny smothered with her shawl,
It isn't any good at all;
Somebody has to pay.
I told you so. I told you so,
I told you something has to go,
Somebody needs to find the dough
And ante up today.

Short change in short, and shorter shrift,
The gunsel sliding from the lift,
The *consigliere* getting biffed,
You get my drift, you get my drift,
You have to take the strain.
For more is less and less is more.
It's what you stole the money for:
The shinbones underneath the floor,
The fingers in the drain.

I know it's never what you meant,
And you're the one that pays the rent.
I wish this wasn't how it went.
I wish some things were different
But that's the way they are,
And I'm the one who digs the dirt:
The bellhop slaughtered in his shirt,
His bottom stuffed with bladderwort,
His mouth stopped up with tar.

He should have done as he was bid,
Have zipped the lip and shut the lid,
But having, as he surely did,
The morals of the katydid,

The wisdom of the moth,
Poor lad, he needed talking to.
We know that, don't we? It was you
And always only you who knew
The Chronicles of Thoth:

A book that chills the soul with dread,
A book much better left unread,
A language of the living dead
Whose voices drive you off your head.
They do, my sweet, they do.
And now we reach the terminus,
Dead calm succeeding all the fuss,
Who's mad and bad and murderous?
It's you, my own, it's you.

British Food

Frenchmen go to the dogs thinking horses and frogs
    Are the stuff you should put in your belly,
And those hordes of Italians, as potent as stallions,
    Chew pizza and tagliatelle.
Though a burger and relish may taste pretty hellish,
    Americans think it the thing.
But an Englishman's soul craves a Toad-in-the-Hole.
    It's a dish that is fit for a King.

You'll be bigger and fatter on sausage and batter.
    The world will admire how you've grown.
You'll be hearty and hale and you'll soon turn the scale
    At the best part of twenty-four stone.
No, you'll leave not a crumb for it's made by your mum
    And there's nothing as good in the shops.
No, you can't get enough of this wonderful stuff
    FOR A TOAD IN THE HOLE IS THE TOPS

Busy Busy

Busy Busy. Things are humming.
Fresh Solutions are Upcoming.
Mechanisms are In Place:
Media Men are Touching Base.

Signs of Discontent are growing.
Crisis Talks are still ongoing.
Market Forces stay On Side
For a Rollercoaster Ride.

Bankers are becoming beggars.
Feisty Girls are falling preggers,
Miniskirts in Minicabs:
Everything is Up for Grabs.

Mullahs make a New Dynamic:
Rectal bombs are Unislamic.
Binge-Drink Cultures are to blame:
Ministers will Name and Shame.

Rolling programmes of Awareness
Mean a Quantum Leap in Fairness.
Premier steers the Ship of State
Through a National Debate.

Living Legend seeking closure
Goes for Maximum Exposure.
Palace Leaks must be addressed:
Prince Charles faces House Arrest.

Back-to-Basics Bishop voices
Need for Change in Lifestyle Choices.
Old-Style Values are the Key:
Marriage and the Family.

Candyman

It was the cruel Candyman
Who came and took my child away.
He locked her in his transit van
And drove her from the joy of day

Into a sad and seeling night.
No moon or stars were in the sky,
He needed none, his eyes were bright,
They lent the light to steer him by.

His horrid hair was lank as rope,
And cold as fish his hangman's hands.
He had no faith, he had no hope,
His life had run into the sand.

So scoured of humankindness, wild
With withering, he took my child.
Pitiless as a metronome,
He wrenched my darling from her home
To lie in some unfathomed combe.

But I will live, if God is good,
To flay his flesh and drink his blood
And grind his bones into the dust,
For that is right and that is just.

Burglars

When you waken with a shudder
in the middle of the night
And the fear is like
a spider on your skin,
Then the faces at the window,
ghastly-gleaming grisly white,
Are the burglars who are trying to come in.

And the burglars in the shadows
of the laurels in the park,
With their sacks marked SWAG,
half-hidden in the leaves,
They are waiting for the children,
they are waiting in the dark,
For the darkness is the proper place for thieves.

Burglars' eyes behind their burglars' masks
are glittering and clear.
They are thinking of the crunching
of the bones,
And the furry, whirry sounds
like baby animals you hear
Are the conversations on their mobile phones.

You can feel them as they fumble,
you can sense them as they scratch,
As those stripy burglars'
jerseys start to itch,
And the stoppered jars of chloroform
for children that they catch
Are all stacked together neatly in the ditch.

Purple strands of skinny cloud
are drifting sideways past the moon
And uncertain stars
are trying not to shine.
Every burglar, knowing children
will be coming very soon,
Licks his blubber lips and mutters, *You are mine!*

You are coming, little children,
in your ones and twos and threes,
You are hurrying
because it's getting late,
You are thinking of your mummies,
you are thinking of your teas,
When perhaps you should be
thinking of your fate.

For we love you, how we love you,
as a tracker loves his tracks,
How we love you as a butcher
loves his hook,
How we love you as a stamp-collector
loves his penny blacks,
As he sticks them in his
stamp collector's book.

Since it's useless to cry out
and quite impossible to run,
It's important that you
follow my advice:
When a burglar comes to get you, you must shoot him with a gun,
And I guarantee he won't be coming twice.

Changelings

Listen, your changeling children are swinging like monkeys,
Hand-over-hand through the leaves of the trees of the forest,
Hugging and kissing and swinging and laughing and singing
Wishes like wings as they flutter and float to the ground.

Feral and faery and wary, the wraiths of your children,
Glister and glisten high up in the skittering sunshine,
Fashioning songs in the swish of the teetering treetops,
Listen, O listen, the weald is awash with the sound.

Songs of the gods of the gongs in the words of the wicked,
Songs of the wrongs of the crocodile spawn of the devil,
Songs that are born in the terrible teeth of the butcher,
Listen, the music goes round and around and around.

Light-bringing Lucifer burns in the eyes of your children,
Satan the Star of the Morning embraces your children,
Darkness has stolen the flesh of your flesh, and your children,
Lost in the fell of the forest, will never be found.

Cogitations at the Launderette

My shirts spin round and round
As earth spins on its axis.
They make a wistful sound;
It sings of death and taxes.
It sings like piping, clyping birds.
I try to memorize the words.

What are the dreams they sell
In paragraphs exquisite?
What is the truth they tell?
What is it and what is it?
The shadow-line of things unseen,
Memorials of what has been.

I liked the way it was,
The to-ing and the fro-ing,
The way it was, because
I see it going, going,
The phantoms of my yesterdays,
Gibbering as they slip away.

My shirts spin round and round,
The earth is turning, turning,
For this is holy ground
And bushes are a-burning.
Bring up the bodies. Wash them clean.
The Lord of Lies and Fancy's Queen.

This is the ghost in the machine.

Cosmic Dust

The eleventh line belongs to Joe Strummer

Universes stretch before us
Scouts construct tyrannosaurus
Bees hum Hallelujah Chorus
Centipede climbs Cotapaxi
Vicar marries Queen in taxi
Alien spacecraft orbits Venus
Russians raffle Stalin's penis
Gas explosion wrecks collider
Vicar marries nun in glider
Grandma locks herself in kludgie
Vacuum cleaner sucks up budgie
Brides like husbands hot and hairy
Vicar marries phantom fairy
Skeleton is royal hunchback
Hungry schoolgirl claims her lunch back
Cracker jokes are getting subtler
Vicar marries Swedish butler
Chef serves prehistoric fish up
Presbyterians bash the bishop
Midgets favour rabbit hutches
Vicar marries bearded duchess
Bullfrogs copulate in chalice
Pandemonium rocks the palace
Bunnies bid for furry fandom
Vicar marries boys on tandem
Every universe is random.

Dead Souls

The dead lie in their linen, white as chalk,
Their noses, lips and eyes are sewn tight shut,
But they can look about them well enough.
And smell, and breathe, and, Lord, how they can talk.

Stark midnight in the boneyard, black as pitch,
Hark to their shrill, inconsequential chatter.
What do they say? The meaning doesn't matter:
A sort of leathery scratchings where they itch.

These parsimonious threnodies of souls
Cast off, cast out, abandoned in their prime,
To dwindle down the corridors of time
Into the shuttering dark, like fading coals.

Alas poor ghosts, on whirring, westering wings,
Too late, too late—it cuts you like a knife—
Tedious in death as tedious in life,
They mourn the lost magnificence of things.

Defining of Terms

Here are three sticks. I set them up on end
Like so. This is my CASTLE, understand?
My castle. It is mine. I shall defend
It with the weapon in my hand,
This other stick. And you shall have this BALL.
Your weapon is this leather ball. You BOWL
It fast and straight to make my castle fall
If I should fail to strike it with the pole
I call my stick, or rather call my BAT.
But if I do, strike it I mean, I RUN
From here to here, a SCORE to me, and that
Is surely clear enough for anyone.
But here's some more. My castle is the WICKET.
The ground we call the PITCH. The game is CRICKET.

If, over time, more men desire to play,
We stand them in the field where we have set
The pitch, to CATCH me out, FIELDERS we say,
To FIELD the ball you bowled I hit. And let
These fielders be your TEAM. I will have others,
My team, who take their turn when I am OUT,
When you have hit my wicket, then my brothers
Shall severally go IN. Then, turnabout,
Your team goes in to see what they can score
Before we bowl them out. When they are done
We total up the runs. The team with more
Shall celebrate with beer. For they have won
The MATCH. And there is little more to trouble you
Before THE ASHES, LORD'S and LBW.

Doctor's Report

It goes like this, the doctor said,
You must lie down upon this bed
Erected in a place apart
And we will open up your heart.
I asked, rebuttoning my shirt,
But will I die, and will it hurt?
He laughed. Don't even think of it.
It will not hurt one little bit.
And for the other, my oh my,
I guarantee you will not die.
A month or two, you will be fine.
I signed upon the dotted line.
He seemed a pleasant sort of bloke.

It did hurt and I didn't croak.

Dreams of H.P. Lovecraft

Cthulhu was pronounced ker-thoo-loo
by Lovecraft—at least sometimes.

Pictures in the stealing dark,
Conforming to an ancient pattern,
Pictures fashioned far beyond
The sixty-seven moons of Saturn:
Withered Murder mumbling in the
Wardrobe with his killer hat on,
Pullulating, suppurating,
Like a spider that's been sat on;
Hear the rhythms of cthulhu,
Beaming out from pole to pole.

Here's a sight to freeze the blood,
To stop the heart and loose the bowels,
Horrid fairies digging, digging
With their little fairy trowels,
Burying a body swathed from
Head to foot in bloody towels,
While they ululate in horrid
Lazar language lacking vowels;
Hear the rhythms of cthulhu,
Like a paraphrenic mole.

Taller than the trees, Behemoth
Of a prehistoric race,
Born to savage bondage, born
Beyond the pale of God's good Grace,
Diabolic-melancholic-
Catatonic carapace,
Creeping through the shadows weeping,
Though he doesn't have a face;

Hear the rhythms of cthulhu,
Pulsing through each vacuole.

No, he doesn't have a face,
Indeed he scarcely has a head,
Tooth and tongueless, heart and lungless,
Eyeless, noseless, polyped,
Polyfilla-caterpillar,
Bitter-critter, better dead,
Shambling up and down the spaces
Where an angel fears to tread.
Hear the rhythms of cthulhu,
Hear them throbbing in your soul.

Dylan Re-dylaned

This was a competition. You start with the opening line of a poem and take in a different direction. I let Dylan have another line and old Bill gets a phrase.

I see the boys of summer in their ruin
And wonder what the hell they think they're doing
The coke they're sniffing and the pigs they're screwing.

Where is the power, the passion and the glory?
Gone to the bad, the same old blame old story.
They're minting money and they're voting Tory.

None of them do the sort of thing we useter.
They haven't got the balls, the jungle juiceter
Behave like men and strut it like a rooster.

Their bolt's been shot. They've gone to pot. They're finished.
The golden glow is little more than tinnish,
Tarnished, unvarnished, utterly diminished.

These boys of light are curdlers in their folly.
They've sold the dream we used to have for lolly,
And scorn the workers' beer to drink the bolly.
Bright day is done. It makes me melancholy.

Elegies for Two English Poets

I.
Let a brooding, black-sailed carvel
Bear the soul of Andrew Marvell,
In its last and sweetest slumber,
On the waters of the Humber,
Out upon the ocean breeze,
Out across the sundering seas,
To those Islands of Delight
Far beyond the encroaching Night,
Lands of Chocolate and Spice,
At the Gates of Paradise.
Andrew Marvell, Yorkshire's son,
Wife and children had he none,
Friends and wine had he aplenty,
Darling of the *cognoscenti*.
Let this solemn passing bell
Ring his valedictory knell.

II.
Let the waters of the Jordan
Wash the soul of Wystan Auden,
Wash it whiter than the snows are,
Though, like leaves in Vallombrosa,
Thick and fast his sins are strewn
Numberless beneath the moon,
Still the followers of his hearse
Honour Wystan and his verse.
Let there be, among the chosen,
Berlin boys in *lederhosen*,
Boys American and English,
Boys so kissable and tinglish,
Angels by the blushing binful,

Just to name them makes me sinful.
Shrive him, Lord. I know you must.
Sweeten Christian Wystan's dust.

Far Away

Captain Nemo scours the sea
Inside his silver fish.
There's none can tell where he may be,
Yet many of us wish
To leave our lives behind and sail,
As members of his crew
To seek the silkie and the whale
Where sextant, chart and compass fail
In oceans far beyond the pale,
At least we think we do.
The skies are fraught, the wind is keen,
The waves are never still,
But Captain Nemo's submarine
Obeys his iron will,
To boldly go and boldly go
And boldly go again
To lands that auks and griffins know,
Where dark, primeval forests grow
And dragons raven to and fro,
Beyond the haunts of men.

Gender Bending

New findings from the City are
That boys are getting prettier,
With breaths most delicate of scent,
With hair not quite as Nature meant,
With sculpted pecs and burnished bodies,
Faces bland as little Noddy's,
Smaller brains and bigger eyes;
The pretty girls, contrariwise,
Though still desirable enough,
Are talking turkey, talking tough
And talking serious careers
Which could go on for years and years.
Economists predict no end
To this unprecedented trend.

G. K's Weekly

Murder most foul is on the prowl,
We have a corpse. We have a room.
He had to die but how and why?
What fingers grasped the fatal knife?
What flutterings of the human heart
Disturbed the silence of the tomb?
What dark designs of Catalines
Have broken up the House of Life?

The questions breed and multiply.
Our quest is just beginning.
Though Sin is endless, here and now
Must be an end to sinning.
When Father Brown hits town then God
Is definitely winning.

The scent of flowers, the strew of verse,
The creak and rattle of the hearse,
The mourners mumbling at the back,
The customary suits of black,
The children's tears, the wasted years,
The whining of the widow's curse,
The will destroyed, the null and void,
The foxes fighting in the sack.

Some eat strange salad with their meat.
Some boil a bitter brew. Some,
Who trade in twine and razor-blades,
Facilitate the gruesome,
But God and Father Brown combine
To make a winning twosome.

There's plenty on the solver's plate.
The suspects all alliterate.
Fenella Fay and Harry Hay
And Damascene Dubois,Duquesne,
They go in threes and, like as peas,
Prefigure turmoil in the state:
Bad Bolsheviks, sad Millionaires,
Professors, most of them insane.

Great Holy shit! He's onto it.
The trail will grow no colder.
Without a doubt he'll smoke it out
Before we're that much older.
For moonstruck, Godstruck Father Brown
Strikes gold in every boulder.

The clues are solved, and most involved
Delight to hear a crime confessed.
A rigorous analysis
Has quite dispelled the mists and murks.
All's clear and nothing is suppressed,
And thus the brightest and the best
Practitioner of quips and quirks,
Old Satan with his hellish works

Has sprung a leak—he's up the creek
And hasn't got a paddle.
The chips are down and Father Brown
Confounds the fiddle-faddle.
Yes, Father Brown is on the case
And God is in the saddle.

God Lite

We don't do God. We've got big numbers now.
The magic zeros replicate for ever
Their demonstration of the why and how
We have cleansed our church of God, being so clever
The mysteries prove unmysterious:
Hell's bells, the mines of sulphur, flames and flails,
Devils with forks and fangs – can you be serious?
We need no tolerance for fairy tales;
Our world goes way, way back, a zillion zillion
Years. And these days there's our First XI
Of Scientific Cracks in the pavilion
Determined to engage the Host of Heaven.
Armed to the teeth with figures, facts and fossils,
We'll devastate His Angels and Apostles.

Night Flying

I am the Sacred Flittermouse,
    The God of all the Gongs.
I've got the skills, I've got the nous,
I do not moan, I do not grouse,
I am the Singer of the Songs,
I am the Righter of the Wrongs,
    And Master of the House.

My Mirrors tell me what I've got
    And where I have to go,
And who is who and what is what,
And stratagem and counterplot.
They tell me what I know I know
And what I say and what is so
    And what I know is not.

God probably does not exist,
    Or if he does he's dead,
Or high, or permanently pissed,
Or on the take, or on the list,
Or off the wall, or off his head,
Or that is what the Mirrors said,
    At any rate, the gist:

A clang of Gongs, a clash of Brass,
    A firmament of Gold,
A kiss-the-book, a kiss-my-arse,
A whisper to the shivering grass,
A tale untrue, a tale untold
(But very strange and very old),
    That God is in the glass.

Frightful Friend

*The italicized lines are borrowed (slightly emended)
from Walter de la Mare*

When your mind is a blank and there's nothing to do,
    When your future is what you forgot,
When you haven't a hope and you haven't a clue,
    When you're steadily losing the plot,
When you're making one hell of a hullabaloo,
    Strait-jacketed into your cot,
He will whisper discreetly, 'Ah friend, is it you?'
    And there's no-one to say it is not.

When it's bonzer, it's beezer, it's tickety-boo,
    And your enemies all have been shot,
When you've dug up the treasure of Brian Boru
    And loaded it into your yacht,
When the master's just massacred half of the crew
    And you have to do something, but what?
He will sidle aboard with his, 'Friend, is it you?'
    And there's no-one to say it is not.

Gray's Elegy Gilberted

If a poet requires his poetical fires
To ignite with improved incandescence,
Then the place and the time he selects for his rhyme
Will turn out to be just of the essence.

He will certainly find his acuteness of mind
(Which results in a language more muscular)
Plus his sense of romance to be greatly enhanced
As the atmosphere grows more crepuscular.

And as to the where, I can readily swear,
I predict a swift end to his search
Should he choose to enthuse his recalcitrant Muse
In a graveyard adjunct to a church.

It's an apothegm sound that the dead in the ground
And the gravestones above them erected
Are subjects most suitable for the immutable
Truths our great bards have selected.

Like the veriest peasant, our ends are unpleasant
Whatever our fame or urbanity,
Shut up in a box with no picks to the locks
All our hopes and our wishes are vanity,

Lord Nelson, Will Shakespeare and Nicholas Breakspear
Who finished his life as a Pope,
The ploughboy, the cowboy, the lowest-of-brow boy
And every anonymous dope,

We are all dead as mutton; when bright as a button,
We think that our life waxes jollier,
Yet the older we grow with the more that we know,
We fall prey to a deep melancholia,

Till we find that our pigeon is old-time religion,
Though once we had jibbed at the thought of it.
WHEN YOU'RE SEVENTY-ODD THERE IS NOTHING
    BUT GOD,
And that is the long and the short of it.

How Can You Believe Me

I know my life has been a lie.
I've been a liar all my life.
I know the how but not the why.

I want to score the perfect ten.
I've been a liar all my life.
I want the what but not the when.

I think the theme but not the thought.
I've been a liar all my life.
I think the thing but not the ought.

I need the where but not the who.
I've been a liar all my life.
I need to stick to you like glue.

I wish the kiss but not the kill.
I've been a liar all my life.
I wish the which but not the will.

I dream the dream but not the deed.
I seek the strive but not the strife.
I know the code. I feel the need.
I've been a liar all my life.

How Pleasant to Know Wendy Cope

How pleasant to know Wendy Cope,
A poet of true popularity,
No dismal dispenser of dope,
But a model of balance and clarity.

Who speaks to the tests of the times
In a language concise and untrendy?
Who is mistress of metres and rhymes?
My answer is totally Wendy.

Who speaks of the woe that is woman
In thrall to the mess that is man?
Who shows her condition is human?
Wendy Cope is the coper who can.

Let me give you a toast in dry sherry
To this model of Faith and of Hope,
With a Charity makes us all merry.
How pleasant to know Wendy Cope.

Joan Hunter Dunn: A Sequel

The wife's off her head and I'm locked in the shed.
When she starts throwing plates I'd be better off dead.
'She's got spirit, my boy, 'quipped her Dad with a grin,
But neglected to tell me the spirit was gin.

Yes, the Army was fine till I stepped out of line.
What a mountain of grief in a bottle of wine!
'A lark after dark in the Park with a cornet?'
'Great Heavens, Carruthers, that's utterly torn it!'

So now I commute as a clerk in the City
Preparing reports for a finance committee,
A screw I suppose and I'm thankful for that,
But it isn't enough for a wife and a brat.

Miss Joan Hunter Dunn, Miss Joan Hunter Dunn,
When we sowed our wild oats, I suppose it was fun,
But at Brighton Saint Peter's I signed on the dotted,
Benighted, short-sighted, short-changed and besotted.

John Maynard Keynes

The extraordinarily pernicious and malignant figure: Murray Rothbard

John Maynard Keynes was a terrible shit.
    John Maynard Keynes was a bitch.
Let's toss off a bumper to John Maynard Keynes,
With his walk like a stork and his head full of brains,
    Who made himself filthily rich.
John Maynard Keynes was a snob and a shit.
Did he know? Yes he did. Did he care? Not a bit.
    He could scratch where the world had an itch.

John Maynard Keynes made a fortune in stocks
    And lost it again in the crash.
But he finished up richer, did John Maynard Keynes,
And he rode round in limos, not buses or trains,
    With a thumping great wallet of cash.
John Maynard Keynes made a fortune in stocks
And he stayed in the game when the ship hit the rocks,
    With a suitcase of gold in his stash.

John Maynard Keynes ruled the roost up at King's,
    Where the world came to sit at his feet.
So he told them a tale, did this John Maynard Keynes,
And they swallowed it whole, silly sheep, plat and plain,
    Giving scarcely a contrary bleat.
John Maynard Keynes was the King up at King's.
As a class they kiss arse, it's just one of those things
    With an upper-crust ruling elite.

John Maynard Keynes was the cock of the walk
    Where he strutted with birds of a feather
He dreamed up a palace, did John Maynard Keynes.
But it shimmered and fell. You can see the remains,

And there's no-one to put it together.
John Maynard Keynes was the cock of the walk
He could smile like a shark and, Lord, how he could talk,
But his talk couldn't alter the weather.

Last Night

The italicised lines are the title of a book by Terence Blacker
about his friend, Willy Donaldson.

Last night I took my life apart
And threw it on the fire.
I stirred the ashes of my heart
Still smouldering on the pyre `
And heard a voice within the fire
Cry out in bitterness:
You cannot live as I have lived
And not end up like this.

Last night I measured out my days
And hid them in the earth.
I measured them a thousand ways
Weighing what they were worth
And heard a voice beneath the earth
Cry out from the abyss:
You cannot live as I have lived
And not end up like this.

Last night I bundled up my past
And lugged it to the lake.
Such a sad farce from first to last
And such a big mistake!
I whispered to the listening lake
As cruel as a kiss:
You cannot live as I have lived
And not end up like this.

Prince, are you there? The thickening air
Begins to smoke and hiss:
You cannot live as I have lived
And not end up like this.

Like

I was a cosmic protoplasmic beetle
Where protoplasmic moss and dross grew tall like
The goddam world was boiling like a kettle
And universes all were very small like

With sun and moon and starshine all a-making
Their seven heavens in the way back then like
Us goddam beetles knew what was a-cooking
The long long view we knew would end in men like

Good god and bless america and hamlet
The primrose path that had to end in art like
Too many goddam eggs to make an omelette
Too many horses put before the cart like

Plod-plodding to the everlasting bonfire
To pandemonium and mortal sin like
A blowsy, frowsy, round the housey fanfare
Us goddam beetles says it's hellish thin like

You follow where your prancing dancing feet'll
To goddam sodom and gomorrah shades like
You should have stayed a protoplasmic beetle
We told you so, we told you so in spades like

Lost Books

*Lost, yes, but they all existed once, though 'The Arthuriad'
only in Milton's head.*

I swear I cannot wait to start
The Romance of the Devil's Fart
By Francois Villon, and I know
The History of Cardenio
By William Shakespeare would repay
Perusal on some rainy day.
Likewise, how good to read, then quote
The racy *Memoirs* Byron wrote,
Franz Kafka's works when but a lad,
John Milton's great *Arthuriad,*
Or Eliot's crafty cavalcade,
Literature and the Export Trade,

Ghostly volumes, cunning, clever,
Vanished, banished, gone forever,
Till released from hugger-mugger
By some learned, longhaired bugger.

Little Chris in the Garden

This is the boy in the sun in the garden and
These are the sights and the sounds of the summer,
The sighing of grasses, the tinkling of water,
The murmur of flowers, the creaking of beetles,
The buzzing of bees and the flutter of butterflies.

These are his sisters and friends of his sisters and
This is the song of them singing, the song of
The wheels of the bus going round, going round, going
Round, going round, going round, going round
In a sussurant pattern of sound all around in a
Sussurant pattern of sound.

This is the boy in his shadowless summer and
This is this sight and the sound of forever,
The boy in his garden of gold.

Lovesong for Bobbie Wickham

A one girl beauty chorus, a pippin if ever there was one, according to
Bertie's Aunt Dahlia, but also with the *disposition and general outlook
of a ticking time bomb*, she'll do.

See the sunshine shining hotly
On the tottering towers at Totleigh,
Shining on a rather motley
Crowd of aunts and girls and chaps,
Stiffy Byng, that utter corker,
Rupert Psmith, the endless talker,
Prudence Stryker, gay New Yorker,
Spiffing girls and sterling chaps.
I know just the way to pick 'em,
I'm in love with Bobbie Wickham,
Lithely, blithely, boyish Bobbie
Sets my senses in a whirl.
Red of hair and fair of feature,
Mother Earth's divinest creature,
Nature's finest, Bobbie Wickham,
You're my sugar, you're my girl.

Linger long in Steeple Bumpleigh;
Though it seem a trifle crumply,
True love here's a *fait accompli*
More than just a vague perhaps,
Lottie Blossom, Kipper Herring,
Nobby Hopwood, deeds of derring-
Do and stolen kisses, this is
So much more than just perhaps.

Spick and span and Bristol fashion,
Bobbie Wickham, she's my passion,
Bobbie posh and oh my gosh
Her daddy's just about an earl.
Snub of nose and long of leg,
Face freckled like a plover's egg,
Yes, you're my pippin, Bobbie Wickham,
You're my sunshine, you're my girl.

Haste to Market Blandings, Salop
Where the jolly hunters gallop,
And the nicest people pal up
At another view halloo,
Corky Pirbright, Bingo Little,
Bonzo Travers, oh the tittle-
Tattle, ah the lovers' prattle
Ttill the time to say' 'I do.'
Heartsick I and like to die for
Bobbie Wickham, bright of eye; for
Bobbie Wickham's roister-doister,
I'm her oyster, she's my pearl.
Ring for Jeeves and Bobbie Wickham,
thick as thieves with Bobbie Wickham,
Aphrodite in your nightie,
Bobbie Wickham, you're my girl.

Hear the pipes of Elfland piping,
Pelham Grenville Wodehouse typing,
Come at last to Basket Neck,
Long Island, hear the siren song,
Pelham Grenville swiftly striding,
Through the shadows softly gliding,

Dreaming English Neverlands,
For life is short but art is long,
Plaiting plots as is his wont, it's
Now you see him, now you don't, it's
Plum entwining Love and Money,
Hear the pipes of Elfland skirl.
Bobbie Pippin, Bobbie Menace,
'Is there anyone for tennis?
Is there anyone at all?' Brave
Bobbie Wickham, you're my girl.

Me and My Shadows

I have a number of poetical akas.

We're old as the hills on our happy pills
And we shovel them in like smarties.
We're woozy and weird with our feardy beards
And our psychedelic shirts.
We're hazy and crazy as oopsa-daisy,
To hell with the arty-farties.
We're cute and we're clever, together forever
In clubbable cymric yurts.

We're sharp as piranhas, we're rhymers and scanners,
The last of the great bullshitters.
We dream so dreamish, so bright and beamishly
Boozing our booze by the vat,
As brisk as the birds with our whirling words
And our doleful, soulful twitters,
Our verses larded with bardic curses
And none the worse for that.

We're fat and we're funny, we're up for the money
And winning the big cigar.
It comes in prizes of different sizes,
From tenners to bloody great sacks.
If we're strapped for cash, and those bardic passions
Will probably mean we are,
With well-turned verses we'll stuff our purses
And yell to hell with your tax.*

Our stretch Mercedes are crammed with ladies
Aas lovely as Dresden china,

From the misty Highlands and islands some,
And some from the beach at Bude.
Our Muses Nine are our summer wine.
There's are none so fine or finer,
Since Aphrodite stepped out of her nightie
And danced by the sea in the nude.

*Prizes are tax-free.

Missed Appointment

The doorbell rang. I caught my breath.
I drew the bolt and it was Death.
He fumbled in his cloak and took
From some recess a little book.
He slid his glasses down his nose.
'It's Mr Whitworth, I suppose.'
A frosty smiled played on his lips
That chilled me to my fingertips,
So I replied in breezy tones,
'No Whitworth here. My name is Jones.'
Whitworth resides at forty-seven,
An ancient shag, and ripe for Heaven,
His mind long gone, his body bent.'
Death nodded, tipped his hat and went.
Jones passed away that very night.
I sent a wreath, as well I might.

Moon Rise

For Gladys Mitchell ('the great Gladys' according to Philip Larkin)
who wrote the book.

What's that cooking in the copper?
What's that bubbling in the broth?
Who's that chopping with her chopper
Something cooking in the copper?
Someone's come an awful cropper
In the Fiefdom of the Moth,
Steaming, smoking in the copper,
Bobbing, broiling in the broth.

You should save yourselves such sorrows,
Stalwart Simon, clever Keith,
More than brother begs or borrows,
So much grief, so many sorrows.
I can trash your rash tomorrows,
Show you such a set of teeth,
Such a a peck of pine and sorrows,
Simple Simon, little Keith.

Prime the pistol, shine the sabre,
Empty out the haversack.
Shrill the fife and beat the tabor,
Cock the pistol, draw the sabre.
Where's your ally? Who's your neighbour?
Keep the faith and mind your back.
Fire the pistol, slash the sabre,
Strikes the hour for paddywhack!

Moulting Beard

Many of the words and images are stolen from Weldon Kees's poem,
'W.K.'s Figure with the Moulting Beard'..

That figure with the moulting beard,
He keeps on showing up in places.
It's scary and a little weird
To see his face in rows of faces
And wonder if I knew him once, and if
I do, is he alive, or just a stiff,

The ghost of a mistake I made
Way back when I was starting out
At what has always been my trade,
Exiting bastards up the spout,
Bastards like him now showing up to bust me.
They mostly had it coming big time, trust me.

There's stuff you'd never tell the wife:
The torch, the poison and the nails,
The lead pipe and the Stanley knife,
The ears arriving through the mails,
The black rain swishing on deserted roads,
The Albanian letter package that explodes,

A street, an empty house, a door,
Downtown Los Angeles perhaps,
Or Brooklyn Heights or Wichita,
And suddenly your whole world snaps,
Because it's him. The fear begins to grow.
It's him, and it's the last thing that you know.

My Boyfriend

According to a discussion on BBC Radio 4, for many teenage girls a vampire represents the perfect transgressive boyfriend.

My boyfriend is one of the undead,
A ravishing sort of a bloke.
His profession is Government funded;
They bought him his fangs and his cloak.

He's dark and he's stark and he's scary.
In graveyards he's specially bad.
But the sun coming up makes him starey.
I think it's all terribly sad.

Him and me are a regular item.
It's me that he nuzzles and necks.
There's a lot of girls wish he would bite 'em,
Cos' they know he's fantastic at sex.

There are hundreds of blokes who are jealous
And claim he's a frost and a failure.
Better button your lip, all you fellas,
Or his old Uncle Vlad will impale yer.

Moonshine

Moon in the water and a sleeping swan,
It's beautiful, you say, and I agree.
It's surely beautiful, and so are we.
And so are we, Quick now, before it's gone,
Let's catch it with a kiss, let's seal it on
Our beating hearts, let's carve it on a tree.
Do you feel it? Yes surely you do. Do you see?
Let's write it in the scattering stars that shone
When life was but a dream and earth a crust
A billion, zillion years before this night.
We love not as we would but as we must;
We know it's beautiful; we know it's right.
Those stars shine still when we are dead and dust.
Whoever loved who loved not at first sight.

Nil Carborundum

Nil carborundum (illegitimis) is dog Latin, on the pattern of the genuine Latin nil desperandum (do not despair). The derivation is (well, of course it is) from the British Army in the Second World War. A carborundum stone is used for sharpening knives and (presumably) bayonets. I have one in my garage—a carborundum stone not a bayonet.

You must never let the bastards grind you down.
   Like a comic when he's funny,
   Like Ibiza when it's sunny,
   Like an egg that's nice and runny,
   Like a bee collecting honey,
   Like a banker stealing money,
Just remember, you're a loser when you frown,
And never let the bastards grind you down.

You must never let the bastards grind you down.
   Like a ghost that glooms and glimmers,
   Like a fairy when she shimmers,
   Like a goulash when it simmers,
   Like the prayers and the hymners,
   Like a shark devouring swimmers,
Do remember you're a hippy-happy clown,
And never let the bastards grind you down.

You must never let the bastards grind you down.
   Like the magic of the random,
   Like a solid silver tandem,
   Like temptations when you've shunned 'em,
   Like intruders when you've stunned 'em,
   Go repeat nil carborundum,
And remember you're the toast of all the town,
   If you never let the bastards,
   Those insinuating bastards,
Yes, you never, never, never let the bastards grind you down.

Notes and Queries

Was Jesus a family man,
A slippers and cardigan feller?
With a gaggle of kids and a van,
Was Jesus a family man?
Did it all go according to plan?
Did Jesus possess an umbrella?
Was Jesus a family man,
A slippers and cardigan feller?

Are traditional males for the chop
In accordance with feminist wishes?
Is the hairy he-person a flop?
Do traditional males face the chop?
Is there anyone wants it to stop?
It's already begun with the fishes.
Are traditional males for the chop
In accordance with feminist wishes?

Are you more of a prick than a berk?
Are you less of a tool than a ratbag?
Are you nuts or just bleeding berserk?
Are you more of a prick than a berk?
Are you less of a twit than a jerk?
Are you thin as a pin or a fat bag?
Are you more of a prick than a berk?
Are you less of a tool than a ratbag?

Orriblerevelationsinighlife

*Planchette . . . wrote down very rapidly an immensely and indeed incredibly long word which was at first quite illegible . . . It wrote it . . . four or five timed . . . and towards the end it was apparent that it began with the three letter O.R.R. I said, "This is all nonsense; there is no word in the English language beginning O.R.R., let alone a word as long as that. It tried again and wrote the word out quite clearly; and it ran:'*Orriblerevelationainighlife.'
—Autobiography: G.K. Chesterton

The duchess is shagging the chauffeur;
How they grind and they grunt in the shrubbery.
Though she sparkles like diamonds of Ophir
In the damps of the snailage and grubbery,
He was always a bit of a loafer,
His physique is pathetically rubbery.

Her daughter is off with the gofer,
But his flesh is revolting and blubbery,
Putting strains on the springs of the sofa
As they couple unhandy and lubbery.
Oh pity the pallid teendaughter
Up the duff when she just didn't oughter.

For this is a tale of the ighlife,
A ballad of pishery-poshery,
A martinis-are-terribly-dry life,
A song of the nibs and the noshery.

I learned of it all at a scance.
On a planchette we used for the Ouija,
A heart-shaped, three-wheelie conveyance
Well-designed for a psychic procedure.
If you keep unbelief in abeyance
I have brought round a message ter read yer

It speaks through the spirit of Fleance,
As white as the bloom aquilegia,
Of true meejumistic purveyance –
I work as a meejum ter feed yer –
Oh pity this meejum before yer,
As broke as a barrack-room lawyer.

Yes this is a tale of the ighlife,
A lay of the lewd and the lecher,
And I'm glad that the bad isn't my life,
Cos such wickedness, where does it get yer?

In a happenstance hidjus, yew betcher.

On Seeing Black Smoke Issuing from the Sistine Chapel during the Papal Conclave

Pope?
Nope.

Out in the Country

I stole the delightful Miss Honey from Roald Dahl

Last week Miss Honey hired a bus
To show the Country to our class.
It seemed an awful lot of fuss
To see an awful lot of grass.

Oh please Miss Honey what are those
Huge hairy things that steam and stink?
The beasts that browse? Oh those are cows.
They give us lovely milk to drink.

Oh please Miss Honey what are those
That walk and squawk on skinny legs?
Along the fence? Oh those are hens.
They give us all our breakfast eggs.

It's very interesting, Miss Honey.
You've shown us heaps and heaps of stuff.
We think the Country's awfully funny
And now we think we've had enough.

Paradelle of the Trees

The grass is down the trees above
The grass is down the trees above
Whispering are up singing below
Whispering are up singing below
The grass are up the trees above
Whispering is singing down below

I of the moon tells me you love
I of the moon tells me you love
She listen everywhere to go
She listen everywhere to go
I me the moon tells she of love
You everywhere to listen go

Like you and me are need the glove
Like you and me are need the glove
A darkness fits to all I know
A darkness fits to all I know
Like I the darkness me a glove
To all are fits you need and know

The everywhere of moon above
She tells me all to like to know
You me are trees are grass a glove
Is whispering singing the below
The darkness fits I listen love
You need the up and down I go

Coda
The trees are whispering up above
The grass is singing down below
I listen to the moon of love

She tells me everywhere you go
The darkness fits me like a glove
And you are all I need to know

Pastoral

The griffin, bodied like a lion, but with an eagle's head,
is, according to Pliny, famed for power and potency.

You're looking very girlish,
In sandals, socks and chiffon,
All gorgeous golden curlish,
So pert and pink and girlish.
I fear it's rather churlish
To stiffen like a griffin
But you're so gorgeous girlish
In sandals, socks and chiffon.

You're definitely boyish,
All tousled-tramp and dirty,
All puddle-jumper joyish.
You seem supremely boyish,
So Bob Hobbledehoyish,
Scuffed shoes and open shirty.
I think you're very boyish,
Tramp-tousled, dirty-shirty.

Then let us go together
Along the leafy trackways.
In rain and sunny weather,
Discovering together,
The flower, fern and heather,
That flourish in the trackways,
The fell of fur and feather
Along the shady backways.

Auntie Phil

I read the wretched wrecks of dreams and hopes.
I trace the tracks of tears, so wan and ghostly.
I see the letters in their envelopes,
And the addresses, neatly written mostly.
You have to keep your spirits up, you must
Preserve the possibility of better.
Your past and future crumble into dust
And yet you find the strength to write a letter
To me, to me. Because? Because to tell
Your sadness and your suffering amends them?
The wounds you bare here never will be well,
You know, I know, we know that nothing ends them.
Something far back, too far, was bad begun.
No comfort save the lack of comfort. None.

Poem for the Oldie

My hands are worse this winter.
My feet are worser still.
My teeth are worsest, by a street,
And every blessed time I eat
I feel extremely ill.

I'm never one to grumble.
Of course I don't complain,
But how I suffer no-one knows.
The agony just grows and grows.
See, there it is again.

I won't last out till Christmas.
I've always been *ill-starred*.
Some might be sorry, come the day
And some might not. It's hard to say,
But not that blooming hard.

No need to send a card.

The Prayer of Harripu Tekojaarvi

God of Earth and God of Iron,
God of Fire and God of Fear,
God of Truth and God of Lying.
God of Living, God of Dying,
God of Sword and God of Spear,
God of Zara, God of Zion,
God of There and God of Here,
God of Kent and Worcestershire,
God of Sorrow, God of Cheer,
God of Leopard, God of Lion,
God of Marduk and Orion,
God of Never, God of Near,
 See my prayer like smoke arisen,
 Free my wishes where they wizen,
 Be the soul of my malison,
 Soon, soon, soon.

God of Water, God of Witches,
God of Air and God of Words,
God of Hedges, God of Ditches,
God of Irks and God of Itches,
God of Beetles, God of Birds,
God of Butchers, God of Bitches,
God of Vocals, God of Surds,
God of all Diminished Thirds,
God of Karshish and of Kurds,
God of Scant and God of Riches,
God of Nooses, God of Hitches,
God of Hermits, God of Herds,
 Take a heart that fears to fly now,
 Wake a heart that wants to die now,
 Make a heart one piece of sky now,
 Soon, soon, soon.

Red Planet Random

Out on the burning, sun-crazed wastes of Mars
Sleeps the Selenian heiress, eyes tight shut.
She had it coming, the galactic slut.
Here's Captain Fergus of the Brazen Cars,
Chewing the seventh of the black cigars
He purchased at some station nissen hut
Beneath the astro-dome. Her throat is cut
From ear to ear. Shit happens in the bars.
Fergus beneath the white, unpitying stars,
Fergus, impassive as a coconut,
Gently massages his policeman's gut.
Unbroken lines of giant nenuphars
Stretch back across the craters. Moonshine bought it
Way back. It flourished. Strange! Who would have thought it?

Who would have thought it? Everywhere the rich
Are getting richer or they're getting shot,
Old Fergus knows how a policeman's lot
Encompasses the fist, the bribe, the snitch.
He needs to catch the murderer of this bitch
And do it pronto. What he hasn't got
He'll have to manufacture. Jeeze, it's hot.
A Martian salamander in the ditch
Starts up a steady, guttural croaking which
Shadows his mood. The Sheriff is a sot
Long married to the bottle. Like as not
He'll dump on Fergus if he sniffs a glitch.
The millionairess is (no, was) a slattern,
But strange and lovely like the rings of Saturn.

Where is the damaged android, whose malfunction
Has turned him to a serial sex offender,

Whose victims, irrespective of their gender,
Are hunted down and slain without compunction
Given a certain planetary conjunction?
Fergus seeks out his secret special friend, a
Dealer in moongrass and a moneylender,
High class purveyor of expensive junk – Shin-
Bone McShane, ex-rent-boy and ex-monk – Shin-
Bone the mystic, magic gender-bender,
Divine Uranian and lost weekender,
Without his help poor Fergus would be sunk – Shin-
Bone the poet, Fergus' one-time lover,
Now a policeman, working undercover.

Relaxation

From Monday to Friday I toil at the mill.
When it gets to the weekend I'm ready to chill.
I'm so fusty and frowsty and sullen and stale
I must go to the ale-house and call for some ale.

So I go to the ale house and call for a double
To go with the ale. Now I'm looking for trouble
And trouble arrives in the shape of a dame
With the face of a Saint and an elegant frame,

But she's straight out of Hell and she's straight out of Chandler,
So wacky and wild that she hasn't a handler,
So randy and dandy and devil-may-care.
I've had seventeen pints and I'm walking on air.

So I'm walking on air so I'm walking on glass.
Then I'm flat in the gutter and flat on my arse
And I'm friendless and loveless and cashless and tight.
But you have to unwind on a Saturday Night.

Rousseau and the Lion

My paintings deal in magic by the metre.
Behold the moon! A lady sleeps and dreams.
She dreams a lion but he does not eat her
As lions do in life. My painting seems

Another life. My lion is not savage.
He is not like the lions in the zoos.
He does not live to roar and rend and ravage
As lions do in life. He does not choose

To be at once magnificent and bad.
He roams the desert underneath the moon.
Regard him as he goes, pad-pad, pad-pad.
The sleeping lady will awaken soon

And play upon the mandolin I gave her.
The lion will lie down as lions do
In dreamlight, softer, beautifuller, braver,
And one day I will paint this painting too.

Rousseau and the Tiger

This is the Tiger and this is Rousseau.
This is the picture I painted to show
That this is the Tiger, so supple and eager.
And this is the customs man, suited and meagre,
And what do we wonder and what do we know?
This is the Tiger and this is Rousseau.

I am Rousseau and I painted the Tiger,
The Tiger so fierce and the Tiger so free.
This is the jungle, the terrible tangle,
And these are the teeth that will torture and mangle,
And all of it up on the wall as you see.
This is the Tiger and this? This is me.

This is the man and he works in an office,
And this is the beast so unhuman and fine.
This is the picture. I painted the picture.
With cunning and craft I effected the capture,
I conjured the colour, I dreamed the design,
And I painted the Tiger. The Tiger is mine.

Seaside Earthquake

Through my telescope on Margate pier
I spy you on the shingle.
All the blood within me seethes and surges
Rround my body's ingle,
As my heart begins to hammer
And my toes begin to tingle.

You're the treasure of the Inca
In Pizarro's storm-tossed galleon,
You're the scarlet Maserati
With its leather-clad Italian,
You're Brunnhilde's thrusting thighs
About her fire-defying stallion.

I've consulted the philosophers
From Abelard to Zeno,
And they say our love is much too much,
But, hellfire, what do they know
As the spark from passion's tinder box
Unlocks my heart's volcano?

Let the lava of my yearning
Start to double and redouble
As the towers begin to topple
And the pools begin to bubble
And the castles turn to sand and
All the promenades to rubble.

There's a grinding from tectonic plates
Of basalt, quartz and granite,
There's a phosphorescent aura
On the ooze that first began it,

There's a red sun setting slowly
On a desolated planet,
And just you and me together
On the darkening shores of Thanet.

Sleepers

Where are the Gods that used to walk the Weald,
Where are their golden limbs and fiery faces,
Divinities of river, tree and field,
The uncommon spirits of the common places?
Where are the gaudy Goddesses of Heaven?
Where are the old immortal sisterhood,
True, talismanic three, or nine, or seven,
Arch-arbiters of evil and of good?
They are dead, you say. Stone dead, you say again.
This wonderful, wide world belongs to men,
And men alone. Show me the bodies then?
I say they sleep. I say they sleep up there,
Inviolate and secret, free from care
Forever, in a better, purer air.

The Song of the Leopard Shepherd

Leopard Shepherd on the Desert is a track by The Underachievers

I am a leopard shepherd
And I shepherd little leopards
By the paradisal river
Where the vine-lined forests shiver
In the jungles of the Congo
Where I sing my shepherd song-o-
Oli-oli-oli-oli-
　Oli-oli-oli-oli-
　　Oli-oli-oli-oli-
　　　O-o-o.

Where the amaranth and moly
Dangle slowly to-and-fro-ly
In their deliquescent clusters
(O the lustres of the clusters!),
With the buzzing of the beeses
In the tall tremendous treeses,
And the chattering of the monkeys
Like a gathering of flunkeys-
Oli-oli-oli-oli-
　Oli-oli-oli-oli-
　　Oli-oli-oli-oli-
　　　O-o-o.

Where the crocodiles are gliding
Up and down and side to siding
In the rancid river water
Where they savage and they slaughter.
There I shepherd little leopards
As a proper leopard shepherd-
Oli-oli-oli-oli-

91

Oli-oli-oli-oli-
  Oli-oli-oli-oli-
    O-o-o-o-o.

Primavera

It is Spring and the young
Are all falling in love.
It is Spring and the tongue
Of the poet is free.
Now Winter is shut
Like a snake in a box
With the shriek of the owl
And the yelp of the fox.
Now Winter withdraws
To his palace of bones,
With a clanging of doors
And a grinding of stones.
And Spring is the kiss
That awakes us again,
In the softness of leaves
And the promise of rain.
So I sing like a bird
At the top of the tree,
The book of the word
And the turn of the key.
I sing like a bird
In the womb of the wood,
The flight of the dark
And the triumph of good.
I sing like a bird,
As the tongue finds its groove
The book of the word

Stolen Kisses

This elfin child was taken into care,
And maintenance devolved upon the State.
His whimpering mother was inadequate,
His father vanished into empty air.
Life came unfurnished – nobody was there
To dress his wounds and make the pain abate.
It was too much to ask and far too late
To find another mother anywhere.
His scars healed up, his head was cleared of lice,
His shorts stayed clean, his nose stopped dripping snot,
But life to him was what he had not got,
And certain of his habits were not nice.
He was a ticking clock about to strike.
Nobody liked him. What was there to like?

Stone Variations

He moved by night. He went alone.
He crept through corridors of stone
Into her reveries of bone.

He'd drawn a blank. The bird had flown.
His friends were fled, his cover blown
And this time he was on his own.

In Peter's Chair the Pope was Joan.
She cursed him in an undertone:
You reap the crap that you have sown.

He wouldn't listen to the crone.
He heard his own testosterone.
Out there beyond the panic zone

The night was right as pheromone,
A scattering of starlight thrown
Across the void of the unknown,

The wind became a sousaphone
Beneath the howling of the drone,
His homicidal chaperon.

Her wildernesses overgrown,
Her staunch, indomitable moan,
He guessed, though he was never shown.

He moved by night. He went alone.

Scrunchy

Scrunch scrunch scrunch went the boots on the gravel.
Creak creak creak went the door in the wall.
Squeak squeak squeak went the rats in the kitchen.
Woof went the hound in the hall.

Moan moan moan went the ghosts in the attic.
Swish swish swish went the folds of their cloaks.
Pad pad pad went their feet in the stairway.
Hoo went the owls in the oaks.

Sniff sniff sniff went the nose of the jailer.
Tick tick tick went the sound of the clock.
Tap tap tap went the friend at the window.
Scratch went the key in the lock.

Drip drip drip went the sweat on your forehead.
Thump thump thump went the heart in your chest.
Bang bang bang went the guns of the soldiers.
Twang went the string in your vest.

Storks

Storks are voiceless and communicate by clattering their beaks

Our stick-legged children muttering like storks,
Hooded, black-coated where the Devil walks,
Tread mystic patterns on unholy ground
And live in strange sussurances of sound.

Smoke from their smokes exhaling like a prayer
Into cathedrals of the empty air,
Whence is their genesis, what their intent,
These convocations of the innocent?

Listen, ah listen. Is it to our good?
Are they behaving in the ways they should?
Are they equivocating and deceiving?
Are their most secret dreams the dreams of leaving?

Stout walking boots raise little puffs of dust.
They stamp their feet to go, for go they must.
They smile like Angels but their hearts are stone.
They are here. They are there They are gone. We are alone.

Teatime in Oxford 1965

It is not as it was to me,
Caesar adsum jam forte.
Translucent china, tinkling spoons
Through long, insistent afternoons,
The lazy buzzing of the bees,
Your proximate and naked knees,
The heady scent of macaroons,
The long ley lines of loony tunes,
The memory of a memory.
The memory of a memory.

Gone with the primps and crimps and curls,
The wide-eyed wondering of girls,
The evasive promises of boys,
It minds me of departed joys,
Gone in the blinking of an eye,
The sift and drift of days gone by.
It is not as it was to me,
It is not as it used to be,
The memory of a memory,
The memory of a memory.

Sweet Song

She didn't love the boy who loved her,
She loved another boy who said
He loved her but he didn't love her,
Loved another girl instead,

Who loved him a while, then left him,
Left him loveless, left him lorn,
She bereft him when she left him
Wishing he had not been born.

In the air the sounds of leaving.
On the sleeve the broken heart.
On the tongue the old deceiving
Overturns the applecart.

Love's sweet song goes on for ever,
Tinkling like September rain.
Love is gone and Love will never,
Never, never, never, never,
Never light your life again.

The Builders

The Empire builders in their khaki shorts
Who painted every continent with red,
Through English Common Law and English sports,
They made the British great and now they're dead.

All of them dead as doornails, dead as earth.
My father in Bombay was such a one,
Selected by no accident of birth,
Cambridge mad dog who braved the midday sun,

Ruling from his Collector's bungalow
Under his sola topee very pukka,
Relaxing now and then to see a show
Or take his pony out and play a chukka.

A sahib and his memsahib, proud and free,
Both young when being young was very Heaven,
And out on the veranda, baby me.
All of this stopped in 1947.

The Lovelorna Song

Lorna Liffen's poem 'Butch Boy' *is indeed about a butcher's boy*

I'm lovelorn for Lorna Liffen
But she's not in love with me
For she only has eyes for the butcher's boy,
For the spiky hair of the butcher's boy.
She's taken a shine to the butcher's boy
And that's how it has to be.

Ah that spliff in the corner with Lorna
At a random rendez-vous!
But she only had eyes for the butcher's boy.
For the earring of gold on the butcher's boy,
She was head over heels for the butcher's boy.
And I don't know what to do.

For if in the sauna with Lorna
I should sigh Love's louche lexeme,
She would still just have eyes for the butcher's boy,
For the fluff on the cheeks of the butcher's boy,
Still shiver with joy for the butcher's boy
In that elemental steam.

You're so simply spiffin', sweet Lorna Liffen,
I dream of you day and night,
But you only have eyes for the butcher's boy,
For the punk tattoos on the butcher's boy,
For the silver chains on the butcher's boy,
For the black leather boots on the butcher's boy,
You're so madly in love with the butcher's boy
That it simply isn't right,
                    Oh no
                         It simply isn't right.

101

The Child on Fire

Our secret games. They never understand.
Oh she was delicate and she was fine.
She smiled at me. I took her by the hand.
I took her by the hand and she was mine.
So small she seemed, curled like a child asleep,
Curled like a fairy in a flower bell.

So small she seemed I could not see her dead,
For how can there be death in fairyland?
Yet she was dead and it was just as well.
God sees. God knows. God knows they always tell.
Though looks like hers would make the angels weep,
She had no part of Heaven or of Hell,

She had no part of pity or desire.
What could I do but put her to the fire?
The fire made tongues about her golden head,
Made tongues of flame and this was what they said.
They never understand our secret games.
God sees. God knows. God knows they always tell.
What was her name?

                    Her name? They don't have names.

The Cuts

It's winter and the weather's dire.
We've no more surplus fat.
Some course of action we require
Before I eat my hat.
Let's throw a granny on the fire
And microwave the cat.

The Dead

The dead come drifting through the floors.
They float and bloat beside my bed,
Snuffling around like carnivores,
Drifting and sifting through the floors
They are not comfortable, these dead.

They crowd into my head and stare.
They gnaw my elbows and my knees.
They tangle in my body hair,
Like a miasma in the air,
A thing that seethes and breathes disease.

They will have blood they say. They will.
Have blood beslobbering their beaks.
They clamber on the window sill.
They wish us every kind of ill,
And chatter in excited squeaks.

They flap like bats, like birds they glide.
They hate the living as they must.
They come at us from every side
Till we have nowhere else to hide
Before we crumble into dust.

The Factoid Multi-Universe

He has been struck by lightning, the unfortunate postilion,
As scorch marks on his skull and feet indubitably show.
Poor Albert Trott once struck a ball clean over Lord's pavilion;
No one has yet repeated this unprecedented blow.
In seconds (twenty billion to the power of twenty billion)
Vile entropy will put a stop to everything we know.

The General Good is not the same as what is good for all.
The mills of God grind slowly but they grind exceeding small.

Praise-God MacArthur got the dumb bum's rush from Harry Truman.
The world, said Wittgenstein, is everything that is the case.
All dragons, snakes and crocodiles fall prey to the ichneumon;
They flee in fear and trembling if they meet him face to face.
I heard it on the grapevine, Elvis Presley was a woman;
That premise granted, many other facts fall into place.

I've quite forgotten where it was I heard it or I read it.
Some stories have the ring of truth and some you'd barely credit.

Black holes are the invention of Professor Stephen Hawking;
The good Lord knows (and no one else) what sort of bill they fill.
Some say God's not a gambler but it's just the whisky talking;
When the Devil drives the tumbrel let the cards fall where they will.
If your name is Long John Silver you must change your way of
  walking
Down that crowd-compelling platform where they take the Train for
  Ill.

There are facts and there are factoids, there is can and there is can't.
There are things you wish were true but they unfortunately aren't.

Why did Gustav Holst equate the horrid Jupiter with jollity –
That double-dealing rapist with his lack of self-control?
Have the Ministers and Elders of the Presbyterian polity
Allotted every sin to its concordant pigeonhole?
Does the world consists of monads, which, though differing in
quality,
Are infinite in number and possess their share of soul?

The Mover of the Cosmos is a monkey in a suit.
There's an information overload; these files do not compute.

You can scry it in the crystal, you can taste it in the water,
You can spell it in the tea-leaves, you can sniff it in the smoke.
Cut out this booze and buggery, invest in bricks and mortar;
A wife and child is what you need to stop you going broke.
Our life is short, the poet says, and yours is getting shorter;
Just what will you have done, my son, before you bloody croak?

The *truth is as we say it is. In God we place our trust.*
Don't meddle. Things could swiftly go spectacularly bust.

The Fishes' Song

Now I am frail and sick and old,
I wander in the winter cold
Beside the lake to watch the fish,
Elusive as a half-formed wish,
And listen to their fishy song:
You chose and you have chosen wrong,
You did, and, see, your every deed
Lies strangled in the waterweed.
Up and down and to and fro
Beneath the ice they come and go,
Beneath the ice their shadows pass
Like figures in a scrying glass.
As evening creeps across the grass,
Beside the trees along the lake:
Your life has been a sad mistake
And all you planned has gone awry.
The whispers in the branches die,
The shadows flee, the sun sinks low,
I wander in the fields of snow
And there is nothing left to know.

The Footfall of a Moth

Listen! the footfall of a moth
Across the kitchen tablecloth,
A weevil mumbling through a crust,
A susurration in the dust,
A silverfish behind the fridge,
The thousand wingbeats of a midge,
Low murmurations of a mouse
Curled up inside your neighbour's house,

Whispering of a daffodil
In bloom on some far distant hill,
Coloratura of a bat
Above a Brighton laundromat,
The grunt of huge tectonic plates
Somewhere in the United States,
A moonbeam's hiss, a breath on Mars,
The sibilance of dying stars,

The music of the spheres, the sound
Of Stygian silence underground,
No perturbation of the air,
But perfect stillness everywhere,
The stillness of a single swan
Upon the lake of Acheron,
Black swan to mourn that love has gone,
When love has gone, when love has gone.

The Furniture

The furniture sat silent in the room.
The wardrobes would not say what they had seen.
The bed was cold and empty as the tomb.
She flicked the pages of a magazine

For information that it had not got.
Where would she go? She knew she had to go.
What did they want? She knew it was a lot.
How would she pay? Ah, that she didn't know.

When would they come? Too soon. She was sure of that.
What was the perturbation on the stair?
Was it the cat? She didn't have a cat?
Why did she feel a thickening in the air?

Why did she startle like a stricken deer?
Why did her eyes look terrified and wild?
What was the twittering shadow drawing near?
Where was the child, the child, the weeping child?

The Use of Biscuits

What is the use of biscuits? What
Have biscuits, in their essence, got
That cakes or crisps or crumpets lack?
The perfect or platonic snack,
Adjunctive to a cup of tea;
Are biscuits all that this might be?
Or are they an irrelevance,
A hypocritical pretence,
A mask, a mummery, a sham?
Do biscuit-junkies give a damn
For values decent people feel?
Betrayers of the commonweal
Of common sense and common good,
Of modesty and motherhood!
Race-hate, date-rape and child-abusing
Can all be linked with biscuit using.

The Immortal

'Please God, let Victor Trumper score a century today against England – out of a total of 137 all out' —Neville Cardus.

Here's to the king of bat and ball;
Let's toast him with a bumper,
The finest cricketer of all:
I give you Victor Trumper.

A man of honour, true and straight –
You read it in his face –
A batsman peerless, exquisite,
True heir to Doctor Grace,

He had the gift, the time, the touch,
The suppleness of limb.
He did not care for money much.
It did not care for him.

Cricket's a science and an art –
So many things to learn.
Cricket's a game – get in, get out
And give your mates a turn.

The Love Bug

The Love Bug will bite you if you don't watch out.
—Fats Waller

Alone in a library a lovely girl
    Begins *The Faerie Queene* of Spenser,
And as she pushes back an errant curl
    The Imp of Poetry attends her,
Squats by her shoulder, whispers in her ear,
Though what he says to her is far from clear.

Perhaps he instructs her in the Rhymer's Art,
    His Course in Seven Easy Stages,
Conjuring *Artegall* and *Britomart*
    From countless crabbed twin-columned pages,
Perhaps he enumerates her secret sins.
Perhaps that's why she blushes and he grins.

He grins, she blushes and she's beautiful
    Entirely – so the poet Auden
Blazoned his sweet boy's ceremonial.
    For Poetry is Holy Jordan
And she is Poetry, of course she is.
Except that verse is lies, and she's the biz.

For she's the Faerie Queene and he's the frisky,
    The rude Mechanic Bottom, waster, weaver,
Wordsmith and manchild, marinate in whisky –
    The Single Malt, the Gay Deceiver,
The Poet's Passion and the Poet's Crutch.
He's onto something but it isn't much.

What isn't much is all he's got, and this,
    The perfect shadow of a sonnet,

Stands for the imperfect shadow of a kiss
    And everything dependent on it,
Counting the moonbeams, swinging on a star,
Etcetera, et-cet-e-bloody-ra.

The Pen is Mightier

The sword is pointier than the pen.
The jaw is jointier than the penis.
The cock is messier than the hen.
The nun is dressier than the Venus.

The leech is goutier than the lemur.
The deed is doughtier than the word.
The shin is bonier than the femur.
The brick is stonier than the turd.

The girl is prettier than the goat.
The sheep is shittier than the lobster.
The scarf is scarier than the coat.
The monk is hairier than the mobster.

The bint is blousier than the baron.
The lout is lousier than the lord.
The hawk is flightier than the heron.
The pen is mightier than the sword.

The Power of Love

When I go walking on the street
My Guardian Angel walks behind.
I hear the rustling of his feet.
I feel the movement of his mind.
His heart is mine. I hear it beat.
My heart is his and he is kind.

I hear the rustling of his feet.
I feel the whirring of his wings.
Be still my soul, my body sings,
Be still, attentive and discreet.
The Love of God is very near,
That sees into the heart of things.

My heart is his. His heart is mine.
We pray for Grace to flow like wine,
The Grace that knows and understands,
Implicit in the touch of hands,
Where Principalities and Powers
Combine to bless our golden hours.

My heart is his. His heart is mine.
Two hammering hearts, four feet, six wings.
Our intercessions are divine.
My soul be still, be still and know.
Our stillness is the port of kings.
Mark as we go. Mark as we go.

The Room under the Eaves

Ascend the winding second stair
To find the room we call the spare.
It's very cold and very bare,
A bed, a cupboard and a chair,
And something rotten in the air,
A touch of evil rich and rare,
Sad spirits, once so debonair,
Now ululate in deep despair –
The roaring boys, the millionaire,
In brass and leather underwear,
Their corpses shaved of pubic hair,
Each penis a boutonnière
It's all a pretty rum affair,
A whiff of some satanic prayer,
A secret no-one wants to share.
Blow out the candle if you dare.

The Sacrament of the Water

The poem addresses a boy of twelve whose life has been saved by the child vampire who loves him. They escape the law together, she in a sealed box. The source is the Swedish film 'Let the Right One In'.

I bit his head off but he had it coming.
He was unfit to live. He had to die.
Blood cakes the calendar. The air is humming.
I tore his head clean off. He had it coming.
The sun is silent and the night is drumming.
The night calls out for Justice. Tooth and eye
Compels this blessed hammer of the Lord
Whose instruments are Fire and the Sword.

Stark night calls out for Justice. Justice answers.
Am I not Justice to the very skull?
Mine is the music moves the shadow dancers.
The eyeless night cries Justice. Justice answers,
Justice whose smoking knife cuts out our cancers,
Binds up the wounds and makes our body well.
I am the Judge. My Judge's robes are red.
I bit his head off and his brother's head,

Then flung the bleeding trophies in the water,
And sported in the sunshine of your smile.
You drew the short straw but my straw was shorter.
I kicked those bobbing trophies through the water.
God and the Right had ritualised the slaughter.
What if the sentence presupposed the trial?
Sometimes the Good reciprocates the True.
Fate spun the wheel. I bet my life on you.

And won: the world in perfect paradigm;
The ravening raven toppled from his perch,

The guilty brothers punished for their crime,
The lovers found, the perfect paradigm.
We two together till the end of time.
I am the Christ. You are my Holy Church.
Our covenant is blood. Contrariwise,
Is flesh, one flesh. And all the rest is lies.

I sit inside my prison of the dark
And meditate on history, and you,
Who, unbrave, braved the terror of the shark.
Inside my blessed hermitage of dark
I meditate the charming of the quark,
Or maybe it's the taming of the shrew.
The force is with you, now we have the force
Spelled out upon my walls by Samuel Morse.

The Seventeen Secret Histories

Emily Bronte invented the saxophone.
Emily Dickinson married a cannibal.
Zadok the Priest kept a Mexican catamite.
Agatha Christie garroted her grandmother.
Reindeer and penguins beheld the Nativity.
Satanists worship the Deity's testicles.
Christobel Pankhurst adored a rhinoceros.
Elvis's penis was pickled by acolytes.
Julius Caesar plays cricket for Middlesex.
Manfred von Richthofen lived as a lesbian.
Robert the Bruce was abducted by aliens.
Erik the Red was immured in a nunnery.
Lord Peter Wimsey was trampled by centipedes.
Paddington Bear was devoured by a manticore.
Shakespeare ascended to Heaven in Wensleydale.
President Bush is a fictional character.
Higgledy-piggledy, nimini-piminy…

The Shrieking of the Spirits

These children are possessed by evil spirits.
Their heads are empty for their brains are missing.
They bare their little pointed teeth like ferrets
And hiss like certain snakes. You can hear them hissing.

Their heads are empty for their brains are missing.
Spawn of Great Satan and a thousand witches
They hiss like certain snakes. You can hear them hissing.
Devils devoured those brains. You can see the stitches.

Spawn of Great Satan and a thousand witches.
Pity them not. They are no longer children.
Black devils ate their brains. You can see the stitches.
Their filthy bodies are deformed and shrunken.

Pity them not. They are no longer children.
Behind each wicked eye there glows an opal.
Their filthy bodies are deformed and shrunken,
Vessels to bear the sins of all the people

Behind each evil eye there glows an opal.
We know they are the source of all our trouble.
We know they bear the sins of all the people.
And so for them our cauldrons boil and bubble.

Because they are the source of all our trouble,
Our smoking knives must carve their beating hearts out.
Because our seething cauldrons boil and bubble
Our smoking knives must hack their grinning heads off.

Thus with our smoking knives we carve their hearts out,
Their hearts possessed of certain evil spirits.
Thus with our smoking knives we hack their heads off.
They bare their little pointed teeth like ferrets.

Hark! You shall hear the shrieking of the spirits.

The Song of the House

This is the song of the house,
    of the gleam that is gone,
Gone in the trail of the mouse,
    in the dream that is fallen.
Gone in the tale of the rise
    and the set of the sun,
Gone in the pale of the sighs
    of the ghost that is calling.

This is the ghost in the air
    of the people forgotten.
This is the how and the where
    and the why and the what and
The fell of the fire and the flame
    in the moan and the mutter,
This the ineffable name
    of the words we unutter.

These are the sighs in the house,
    unweeting, unwitten,
Whose silences speaks to the mouse
    of the boundless unwritten.
This is the soul of the set
    and the rise of the moon,
And the scroll of the last cigarette
    in the vast picayune.

The Song of the Toad

Last night I dreamed a dream. I stood
Inside the margin of a wood.

Before me was a clearing where
I felt a trembling of the air

And knew that I was not alone.
A man as cold and pale as bone

With silver eyes and locks of flame
Stood in the way and called my name.

He was as tall as forest trees.
His face was heavy with disease.

His voice rang out across the grass
As clangorous as broken glass.

Behold what you must surely be.
Join heart and hands to dance with me.

I am the image of your sorrow
And my today is your tomorrow.

Strait is the gate. The way is narrow.
I am the Corpse within the barrow.

I am the Death within the Tarot.
I am the Toad beneath the harrow.

Grunchle grinchle grobbley greejun.
Gurgle urgle cootchi keejun.

I am the Toad. My name is legion.

The Soul

The soul is like a little mouse.
He hides inside the body's house
With anxious eyes and twitchy nose
As in and out he comes and goes,
A friendly, inoffensive ghost
Who lives on tea and buttered toast.
He is so delicate and small
Perhaps he is not there at all;
Longheaded chaps who ought to know
Assure us it cannot be so.
But sometimes, as I lie in bed,
I think I hear inside my head
His soft ethereal song whose words
Are in some language of the birds,
An air-borne poetry and prose
Whose liquid grammar no-one knows.
So we go on, my soul and I,
Until, the day I have to I die,
He packs his bags, puts on his hat
And leaves for ever. Just like that.

Year of the Bears

That was the year the Fuzzy Bears,
Abandoning their wild confreres,
All set up house beneath the stairs.

Beneath the stairs they made their lairs
And lived an idyll free from cares,
Some solitaires and some in pairs.

The stairs supplied their thoroughfares
Where, jubilant as millionaires,
They flashed their sportive derrieres.

Ah, what a perfect life was theirs,
Beneath the stairs, these debonairs,
Insouciance and going shares,

Those bears, those ursine Fred Astaires,
Nectareous as boutonnières,
Prithee, remember in your prayers

In other times and other wheres,
The bears, the bears, the Fuzzy Bears!

Twitterature

1.
Time Remembered. Had a ball.
Buggery& bugger all.
Tedium beyond belief
Anglicised by Scott Moncrieff.

2.
Liz Bennett's a honey
Who's witty & sunny.
She fancies rich Darcy
Who acts pretty arsy.
But Liz does the biz.
He is hers. She is his.

3.
Old black guy weds young white chick,
Speechifies, gets jealous quick.
Old black guy kills young white wife,
Speechifies & ends his life.

4.
Son sees Ghost Dad.
Ghost says King bad.
'Kill King!' says Ghost.
'Will co!' King toast.

5.
Macbeth meets three witches. The sonovabitch is
Persuaded. Kill Duncan. He does & he's sunk &
Macduff stabs him dead & cuts off his head.

6.
God makes nothing into something.
God sends Son in who gets done in.
God makes Church for more research.
How it pans out is still in doubt.

Variation on a Forgotten Theme of James Fenton

I heard a bird sing sweetly.
I heard a bird sing long.
This, word for word, is what I heard
Of her sweet song:

   Wrong today.
   And wronger tomorrow,
   And wrongest the day after that.

   Broke and broker.
   You take out the the joker
   And put in the aristocrat.

   Nine Hail Marys
   Away with the fairies.
   Remember to put out the cat.

   Dead as a door
   Nail, a coffin or floor
   Nail, dead as a warfarin'd rat.

   This is the sum of it.
   Nothing will come of it.
   Tell him to shit in his hat.

It was a bird of clockwork,
With interlocking plates,
And was the private property
Of William Butler Yeats.

Voices

It's lonely in the garden here, there's no-one but the cat.
There's nothing but the footsteps and you've had enough of that.
You know they're out to get you now, you know they're on your case.
It's starting to unwind, you know they're bound to play the ace.
> *You know they're on your case.*
> *You're just a waste of space.*

It's lonely in the garden here, there's no-one but the snails
Criss-crossing in the darkness leaving phosphorescent trails.
You know they'll never let you go; you're just a waste of space.
They're out to rob your blind, you know they're barely off the pace.
> *You're just a waste of space.*
> *You know they're on your case.*

It's lonely in the city here, there's nothing but the stones,
The echoes in the shadows and the rattle of the bones.
You plead to Heaven for succour and you cry to God for grace.
It's something in your mind, you know its insolent embrace.
> *You cry to God for grace.*
> *You're gone without trace.*

It's lonely in the city here, there's nothing but the tombs.
You give an inch, they take a yard: they're in your sitting rooms.
You don't trust any fucker or you're gone without a trace.
They're never far behind, you know they're cutting to the chase.
> *You're gone without trace.*
> *You cry to God for grace.*

It's lonely in the universe, there's nothing but the stars;
They hum about their courses like celestial trolley cars.
There isn't any time, they said, there isn't any place.
They're scarcely humankind, you know they're from another race.
There isn't any place.
You'll soon be face to face.

It's lonely in the universe, there's nothing but the God.
I knew him when his brother was a crawling chilopod.
You know the voices in your head, you know the heart's grimace,
The footsteps in your mind, you know you'll soon be face to face.
They're always on your case.
They're always on your case.

What are the Gods of the Godless?

What are the Gods of the Godless?
Cigarettes, whisky and beer,
    Banknotes and cheques,
    A whole lot of sex,
An effortless stellar career,
But nothing too chaste or austere.
Yes, these are the Gods of the Godless.

Where are the Faiths of the Faithless?
Youth that continues for ever,
    Fortune and fame,
    Making your name,
By being amusing and clever
With no intellectual endeavour.
So pardon the Faiths of the Faithless.

Consider the Souls of the Soulless
Lost in Dickensian childhoods,
    Pray for the do-able,
    Endless renewable
Greenery-yallery mildhoods,
Not daring a life in the wild woods.
Ah pity the Souls of the Soulless.

Give Gorm to the totally Gormless,
Vacuous, fatuous, formless,
    Grace to the Graceless,
    A face to the faceless
And warm the cold hearts of the warmless,
The shrivelling hearts of the warmless.
Yes, warm the sad hearts of the warmless,

Wicked

I'm wicked. Such a wicked person,
In all the world there's not a worse 'un.
My wickedness is so primeval
I swear I'm absolutely evil
And so unutterably horrid
Horns have sprouted from my forehead.
I clop around on devil feet,
With devil forks I spear my meat,
Then tear it in my devil jaws.
My nails are black, and curved like claws.
My teeth are jaggy like a shark.
I jump on people in the dark.
I roll my devil eyes about,
And, with my wicked devil shout,
Yell dreadful, doomy, devil things.
I've got these pterodactyl wings,
And poisonous snakes instead of hair
(You might not see them but they're there),
I'm wicked and I just don't care.

Wittgenstein's Show and Tell

All I can do is show a thing and say
This is what human life is like, or so
It seems to me, or so it seems to me
That that's the way of things, the way they go.
What do you think? Say yes if you agree,
Smile and say yes. All I can do is show
The way it seems, or so it seems to me.
The play's the thing. So watch the bloody play.

This is what life is like. This is my life.
My life, your life, our lives, they're all the same,
Like chalk and cheese, sweet jeez like day and night,
Like mad and not mad yet, like wrong and right.
Smile and say cheese, sly smiler with the knife.
My life is wrong but that is not the game.

Wiittgenstein's Beetle

My mind is like a beetle in a box.
I open up the box to see it go.
It scuttles up and down and to and fro,
Telling me everything I want to know.
You have to be a hedgehog or a fox.
My mind is like a beetle in a box.

My universes are unnumbered clocks
And every one displays a different face
For each exigency of time and space,
Another person and another place,
Another bastard set of building blocks.
My mind is like a beetle in a box.

Beached and benighted by a paradox,
Our age has lost the concept of degree.
I grieve for it myself incessantly.
If you weren't you who would you wish to be?
You love the freedoms, can't abide the frocks.
My mind is like a beetle in a box.

Pull down your knickers or pull up your socks.
It's sex or standards and I don't care which.
Now is decision time (the rest is kitsch)
And plans for getting seriously rich
Despite portfolios of falling stocks.
My mind is like a beetle in a box.

Is it Christ's blood or whisky on the rocks?
Is it the answer or the seventh clue?
Is it the angel or the bugaboo?
Who would you wish to be, if you weren't you?

Is it the upsurge or the aftershocks?
My mind is like a beetle in a box.

Tick-tock. Tick-tock. Throw out those bloody clocks!
But yours and yours and yours are just the same.
We're on a losing streak. We play the game.
The whole thing's fucked and nobody's to blame.
They're digging down behind the hollyhocks.
My mind is like a beetle in a box.

They sank the blackened bodies in the docks
Which previously were given to the flame.
Who went is clear, a good deal less who came;
It all comes down to claim and counter-claim,
A neat solution, if unorthodox.
My mind is like a beetle in a box.

Yearnings for the Secret Heart

God made a child of mud and blood
And tempered it with fire and flame.
Into the mouth he blew the wind.
Into the eyes he washed the rain,
And gave the child a secret name.

God took the child that he had made,
And found a cavern in a wood.
God hid the wood within the wild
And hid the bad within the good
And hid the heart within the child.

And when the heart began to beat
Within the child, this child of mud,
Began to stir, began to speak,
Began to build a wall of words,
And all the words were words of blood,

Then god who made the child began
To fear that he had made a man,
And dug forthwith a little grave,
And in the grave he placed the child,
And covered it with fallen leaves.

God left the cavern in the wild,
A swirl of stars and God was gone.
The leaves had covered up the child
And yet the heart went beating on,
When God was gone, went beating on.

You and the Universe

The planets and the stars were not aligned
In any other universe but this.
It was much easier for them to miss,
Their molecules to scatter, not to bind,
For every other universe was blind,
They did not see you there to touch, to kiss.
You were not there to see, no synthesis
So proper and convenient to my mind.
But here we hear the trembling of the spheres,
As underneath my hand your beating heart
Beats out in time the time till we must part.
We listen to the whispering of the years,
Like leaves that rustle in a wind that blows
From here to there, to planets no-one knows.

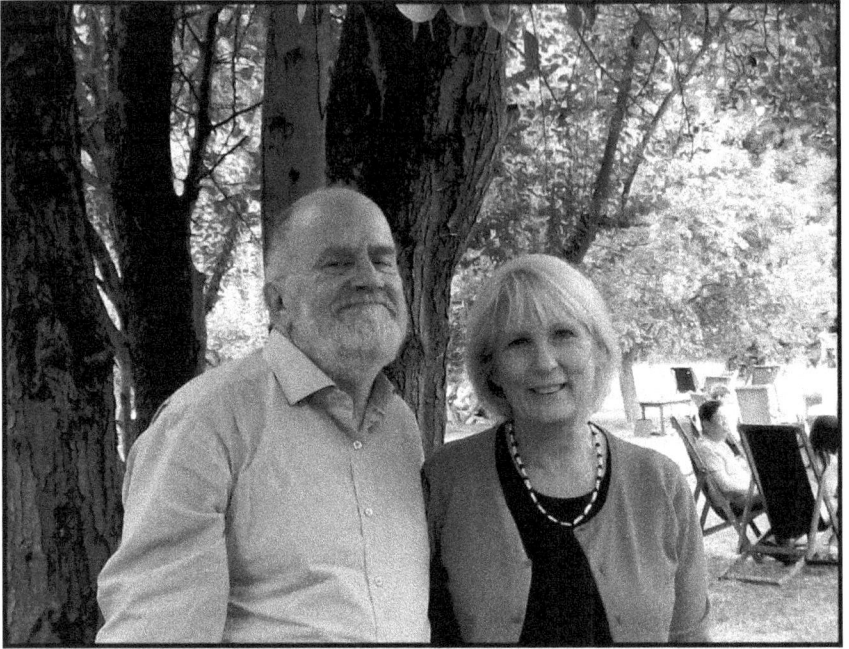

John Whitworth and Karen Kelsay, Editor

About the Author

I was born in India in 1945. I lived as a small child in north London and as a slightly larger child in Edinburgh where I went to the Royal High School. Rather to my surprise I got in to Oxford University and later lived in London and in Canterbury teaching a variety of things. I am married to Doreen Roberts and we have two daughters, Ellie and |Katie and two cats.

But that is not really the point, is it? Why do I write? Why do I write *poetry*. Because I can't write anything else. I have tried writing novels but it didn't work out. What kind of poems. This kind. The kind you find here. Poems that rhyme and scan. Old fashioned poems. I have tried to write other kinds, but like the novels it didn't work out.

I was quite a late starter. No poems at school. It was a fine school but not that sort of place. Bad poems at university. Lord, how bad! But I courted a girl at university (is that really the word?) by leaving silly rhymes on her typewriter. It didn't work out, but she wrote to me later and said she was doing a book of Oxford poets but the stuff she had was too serious. Could she use some of my silly rhymes?. Could she? I got five pound from a real London publisher, Sidgwick and Jackson, and I thought of framing the cheque but in the end I cashed it and began sending stuff to little magazines. It took a long time and a lot of rejections. But in the end I had my second slice of luck. At a big party for an anthology I met Anthony Thwaite and he (drunkenly) asked me to send a load of poems to him at Secker and Warburg, another London publisher. A long time later, it seemed to me, a book appeared, Unhistorical Fragments. I thought I had it made. I didn't but I plodded on and more books followed, none of them selling an awful lot, except for a children's book, which did very well. And I still go on. Publishers sacked me, publishers died, publishers had nervous breakdowns. One publisher had such long queues of poets that I felt death would intervene, his or mine. So here is a book from my fifth one. I hope you like it.

Most of the poems here have been published, most of them for money, not big money, though I once got £5,350 for a single poem, courtesy of the Mail of Sunday, bless them. I enter competitions all the time and sometimes I win. The poems still come. That gives me great pleasure. I feel I am writing my best poems now, though others may not share that opinion, of course. I hope you do.

Books by John Whitworth

Unhistorical Fragments: Secker 1980
Poor Butterflies: Secker 1982
Lovely Day for a Wedding: Secker 1985
Tennis and Sex and Death: Peterloo 1989
Landscape with Small Humans: Peterloo 1993
The Complete Poetical Works of Phoebe Flood (for children):
  Hodder 1997
From The Sonnet History of Modern Poetry: Peterloo 1998
The Whitworth Gun: Peterloo 2002
Being the Bad Guy Peterloo 2007
Girlie Gangs Enitharmon 2010
Writing Poetry A&C Black 2001 reprinted 2006
The Faber Book of Blue Verse (editor) 1990 reprinted 2006

I have copies of all these books to sell. They are also available from
Amazon. But not signed.

www.ingramcontent.com/pod-product-compliance
Lightning Source LLC
Chambersburg PA
CBHW071805090426
42737CB00012B/1959